Grandpa Whe..

A Sensitive Look at Dementia

Nealie Rose

Illustrated by D. A. Pierce

Grandpa When - Nealie Rose

© Copyright 2014 All Rights Reserved

Jari LLC

Used only by permission.

www.nealierose.com

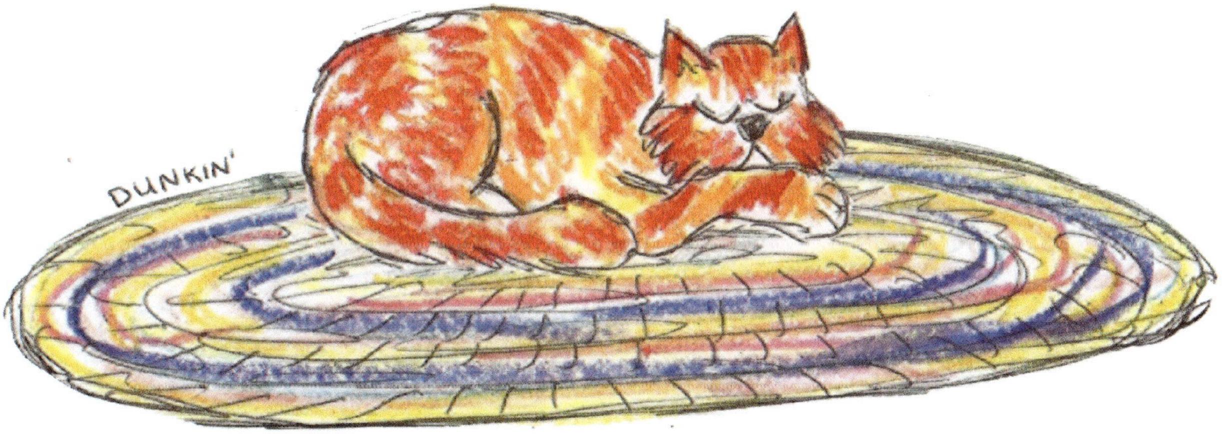
DUNKIN'

Grandpa When   Mommy Why

Me Who   What Bob

What Bob and **Me Who** wanted to visit **Grandpa When**.

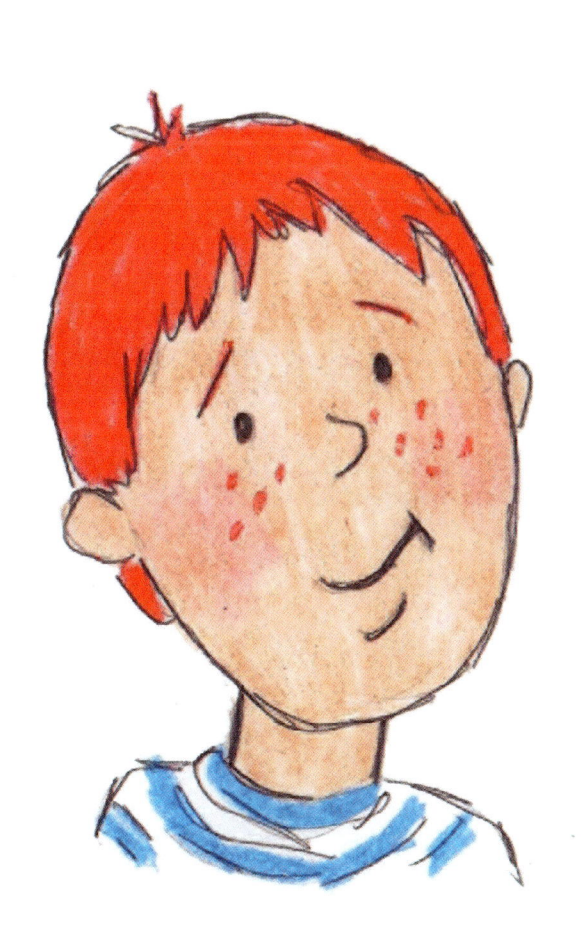

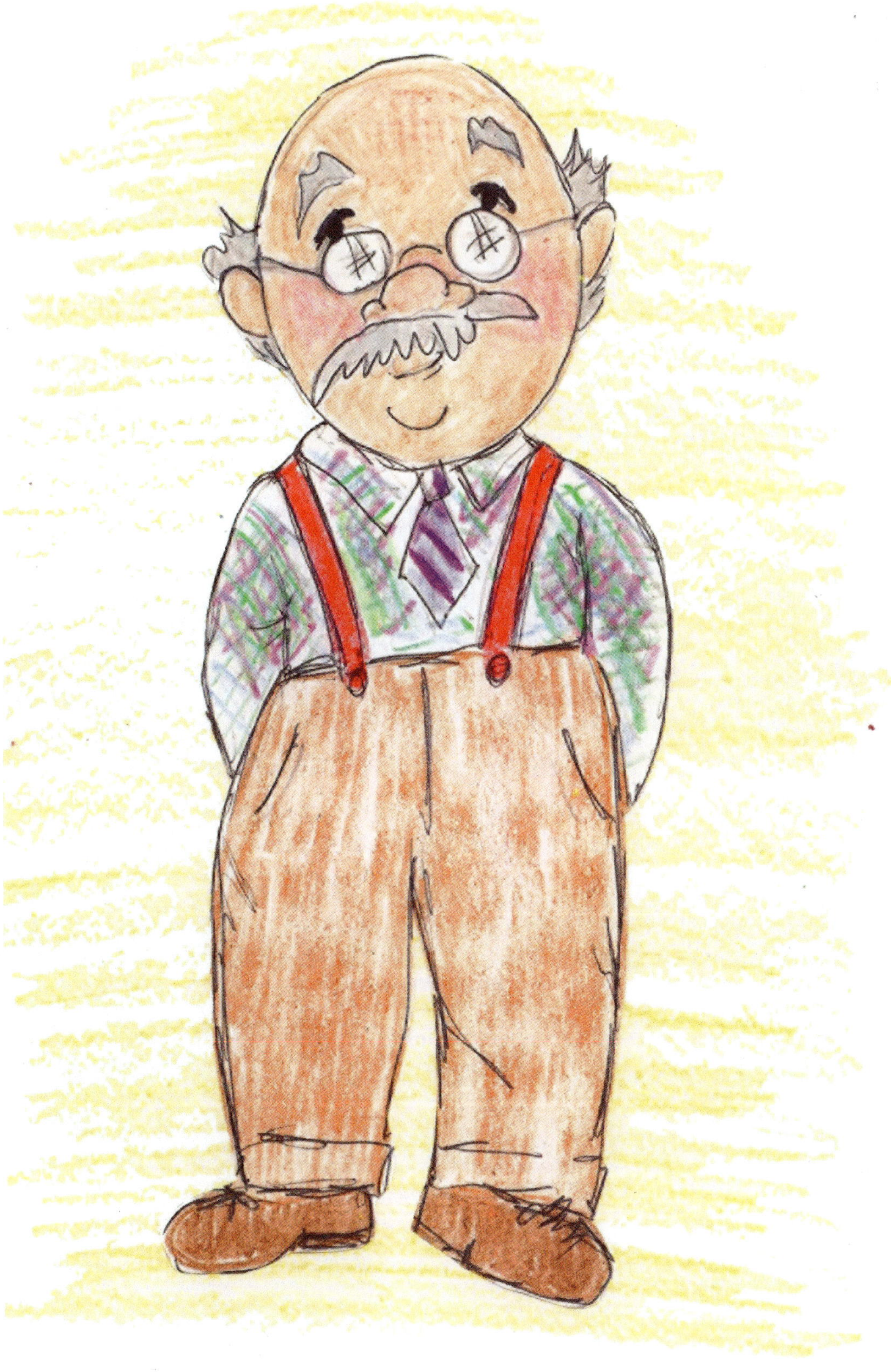

Mommy Why said it had been since last November that **Grandpa When** began not to remember.

Me Who was worried.

"Will **Grandpa When** know me?"

Mommy Why answered, "**Me Who**, be prepared, because **Grandpa When** can't seem to remember anything since last November."

What Bob patted **Me Who**'s head. "Didn't you hear what **Mommy Why** said?"

Me Who frowned. "I heard what **Mommy Why** said. I just can't get it in my head. Will **Grandpa When** see me? Will **Grandpa When** think I'm simply not there?"

Mommy Why answered, "**Grandpa When** will see you, **Me Who**, but he may ask, 'And just **who** are you?'"

What Bob asked, "Well, what should we say if **Grandpa When** asks that of us two?"

Mommy Why smiled. "You must tell **Grandpa When** who you are, **What Bob** and **Me Who**. He MAY look at you and order you out, but remember, it's just because **Grandpa When** has been confused since November."

Me Who asked **Mommy Why**, "How come **Grandpa When** was confused since November?"

Mommy Why shook her head and said, "Nobody knows, **Me Who** and **What Bob**. Be kind to him, though, if he doesn't remember."

What Bob whined, "Can't we just stay home? Don't you see, **Mommy Why**, I don't want **Grandpa When** not to know me and order me out. I don't know what I'll do if I hear him shout."

Me Who added, "Now WHY should we go to see **Grandpa When**?

I think **What Bob** is right. I want **Grandpa When** to know who I am, not think I'm **Joe What** or **Who Cam**."

Mommy Why said, "**What Bob** and **Me Who**, you KNOW who you are, and that will do. When we get there, no matter what you two find, hug **Grandpa When** if he'll let you, and leave love behind.

Grandpa When is still **Grandpa When**, **What Bob** and **Me Who**. Even though he's been confused since November, he will always be ours to love and remember."

Me Who and **What Bob** looked right at each other.

"I guess I can do this," **What Bob** said to his brother. "We will be brave and listen to mother."

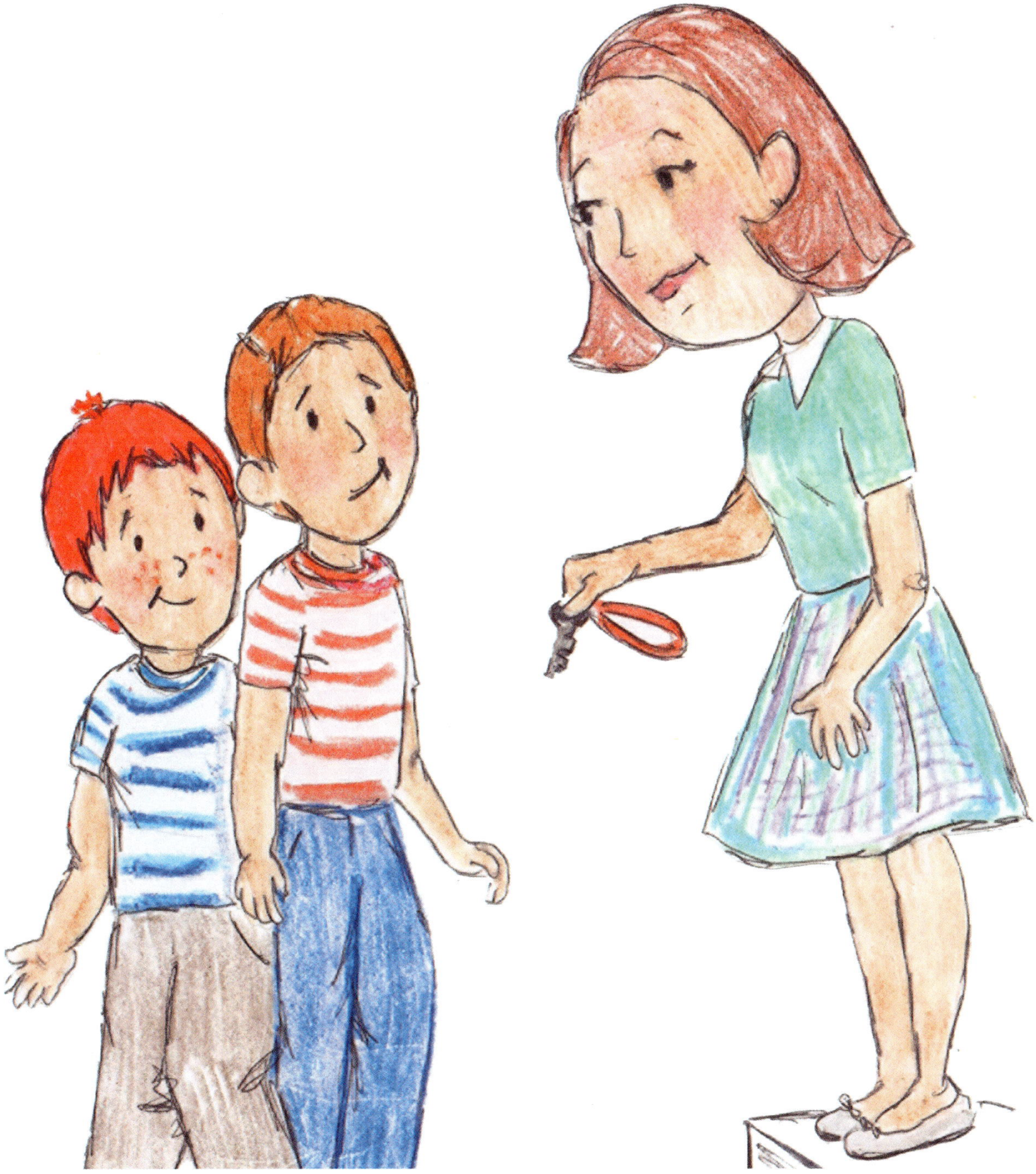

"Okay," said **Me Who**. "We'll go and we'll see. What happens is what happens, and I'll know it's not me. If **Grandpa When** forgets us and orders us out, I will not cry if I hear him shout."

"That's right, **Me Who** and **What Bob**. Put on a brave face and let's do our job. Our job is to love him and always be kind. We'll hug him if he lets us, and we'll leave love behind."

Things to Talk About:

Do you have someone in your life like Grandpa When?

Who is it?

How do you feel about their confusion?

How can you be brave?

How can you show love to that person?

Do you need special help to feel safe around them?

What would make you feel safe?

Who can you talk to about this?

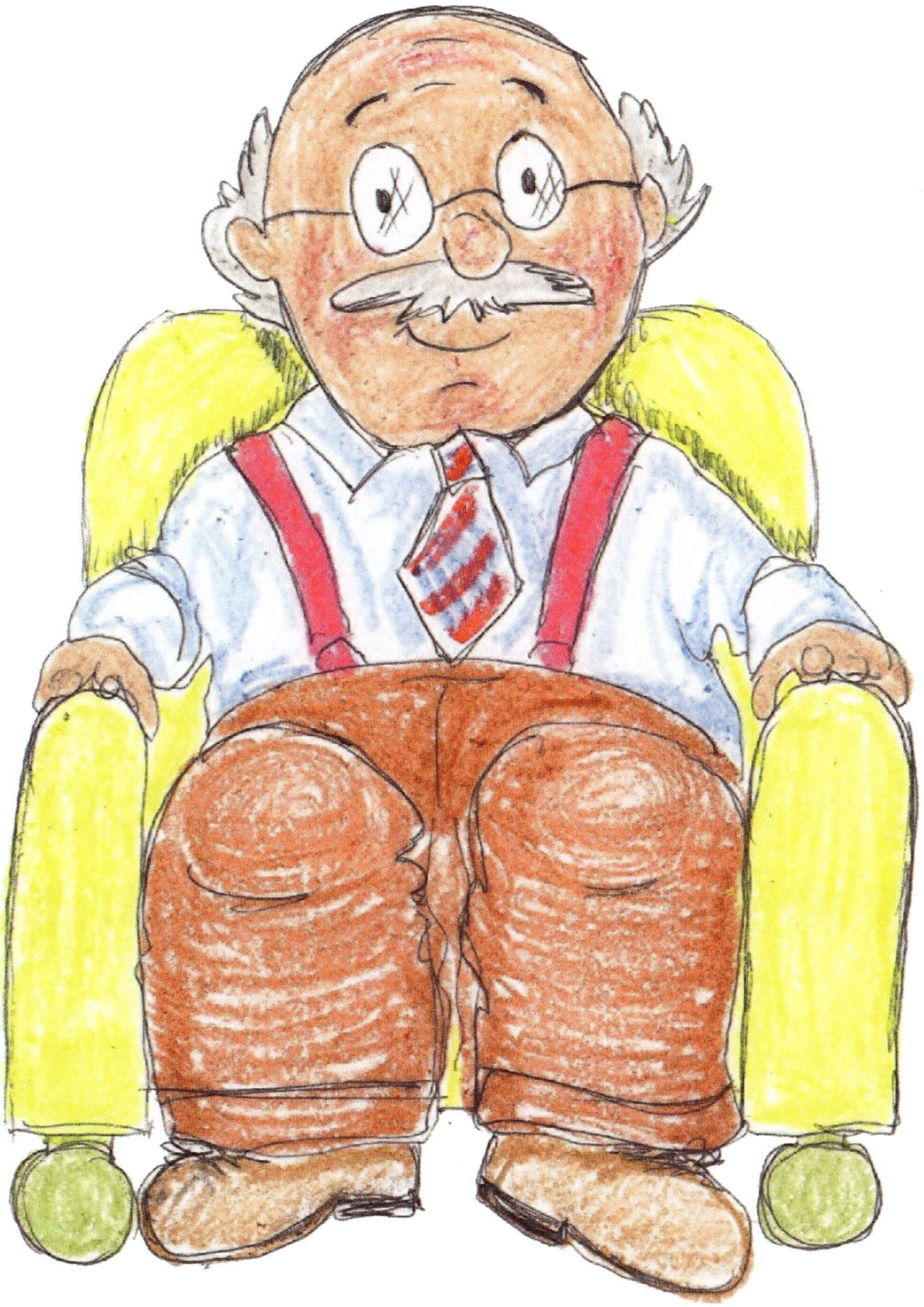

Grandpa When - Nealie Rose

© Copyright 2014 - All rights reserved/Jari LLC

www.nealierose.com

Love Grandpa When...

Printed in Great Britain
by Amazon